Vintage Radios

A Collector's Guide to Timeless Sound and Style

Neal Parker

Vintage Radios
A Collector's Guide to Timeless Sound and Style

Neal Parker

Copyright © 2025 by Neal Parker

All rights reserved.

No portion of this book may be reproduced in any form without written permission from the publisher or author, except as permitted by U.S. copyright law.

For those who still believe in the quiet
magic of turning a dial,
and for every voice that ever echoed through
the warm hum of a glowing tube—
this book is for you.

To my father, who first taught me to listen,
and to every collector who knows that some
treasures don't just speak...
they sing.

—Neal Parker

Introduction

Vintage Radios: A Collector's Guide to Timeless Sound and Style

There's something undeniably magical about the warm hum of a vintage radio coming to life. The soft glow of its dial, the gentle crackle of static giving way to music or voices from another time—it's a sensory experience, a tactile reminder of when craftsmanship, style, and storytelling met in the heart of the home. Long before podcasts and streaming services, families gathered around these carefully crafted machines, tuning in to the outside world with eager ears and hopeful hearts.

Vintage radios are more than old electronics. They are design statements, cultural time capsules, and marvels of mechanical and electrical ingenuity. Their wood-grained cabinets and Bakelite curves evoke mid-century living rooms and wartime kitchens. Their knobs, dials, and tubes still pulse with life when coaxed into operation—quietly broadcasting echoes of the past through their aged speakers. To hold one is to hold history, not in the abstract, but in something you can switch on, hear, and admire.

Despite the rapid pace of modern technology, vintage radios continue to capture our imagination. Perhaps it's their design—sleek, elegant, purposeful in a way that feels both nostalgic and enduring. Perhaps it's their sound—warm and slightly imperfect, a far cry from the sterile clarity of digital audio. Or perhaps it's simply the stories they carry. Each one has lived a life. Some played swing music during the 1940s, while others shared the moon landing in '69. Some sat quietly in garages for decades, waiting to be discovered and restored by someone who could see their beauty beneath the dust.

This book was written for those people. For the curious listener who stumbles upon a radio at an antique fair and wonders if it still works. For the passionate collector who's spent years seeking rare models and restoring them to glory. And for everyone in between—because collecting vintage radios doesn't require expertise or deep pockets. It requires curiosity, a willingness to learn, and a love for the charm of analog sound and design.

Inside these pages, you'll find everything you need to begin or deepen your journey. From the earliest crystal sets to the golden age of tube radios and the sleek rise of transistor models, we'll explore how technology and design evolved together. You'll learn how to identify iconic styles, recognize valuable models, restore old beauties, and build a collection with both heart and strategy. Along the way, you'll meet the brands that shaped radio history and discover the vibrant community of collectors, restorers, and enthusiasts keeping this rich legacy alive.

So whether you're here to rekindle a memory, rescue a forgotten treasure, or simply fall in love with a new (old) hobby, welcome. Turn the dial, adjust the antenna, and settle in—because the world of vintage radios is waiting to be rediscovered, one beautiful broadcast at a time.

Chapter 1: The Evolution of Radio Technology

Vintage Radios: A Collector's Guide to Timeless Sound and Style

The story of vintage radios begins not with sound, but with silence—with the invisible waves that filled the air long before we knew how to listen. In the early 20th century, when the world was still marveling at the lightbulb and the automobile, a new frontier emerged—one that would revolutionize communication, culture, and eventually, the way we experienced music, news, and human connection.

Long before the golden glow of dial lights or the comforting hum of a warming vacuum tube, there were crystal sets. Simple, wire-bound contraptions, often built by hand in garages and workshops, these early radios required no electricity, no batteries—just a crystal detector, a coil of wire, and a pair of headphones. They offered the magic of tuning into the unknown, of hearing voices and melodies travel invisibly across great distances. For many, it felt like capturing lightning in a bottle.

As the 1920s dawned, radio transitioned from experimental hobby to national obsession. The crystal set gave way to the vacuum tube, and suddenly, radios could do more than whisper through headphones—they could speak aloud. Families gathered around their wooden sets, not just to hear music but to be part of something bigger. News bulletins, presidential fireside chats, serialized dramas, big band concerts—all poured from the cloth-covered speakers, shaping a shared cultural experience. In an era before television, radio was the hearth around which society gathered.

The 1930s and 1940s ushered in what many collectors call the Golden Age of radio. Vacuum tube technology matured, and radios grew more reliable, more powerful, and far more beautiful. Manufacturers began crafting radios not just as appliances, but as furniture—objects of pride designed to grace a living room or kitchen counter. Art Deco cases with bold geometry and chrome trim, glossy Bakelite bodies in deep maroon or butterscotch, and elegant wooden consoles with cathedral arches became common sights in homes across the world. Radios didn't just deliver content—they embodied style.

World War II temporarily slowed civilian production, as factories pivoted to military needs, but it also demonstrated the vital importance of radio as a tool of coordination, morale, and information. Soldiers carried field radios into battle. Families back home clung to broadcasts for word from the front. When the war ended, radio returned to domestic life with renewed vigor—smaller, sleeker, more colorful. Post-war models reflected an optimistic, forward-looking world, embracing space-age design cues and vibrant plastics, preparing for an era of mass communication and high fidelity.

Then came the revolution of the transistor. In the mid-1950s, engineers succeeded in replacing bulky vacuum tubes with compact, energy-efficient transistors. Radios no longer needed to be anchored to the wall or warmed up like an old car engine. They became portable—radios you could slip into your pocket, take to the beach, or carry on a walk. This shift changed not only how radios were used, but how they were designed. The era of portability had begun, and with it, a new phase in style and accessibility.

Design, of course, evolved alongside the technology. While early radios prioritized performance, the mid-century era celebrated innovation and individuality. Cabinet designs grew more experimental. Scandinavian minimalism, mid-century modern lines, and space-age motifs influenced both form and function. Color palettes expanded. Dials became more playful. Radio was no longer just a medium—it was a lifestyle.

Yet, even as radio continued to evolve, television began its ascent. By the 1960s and 70s, the living room's attention had shifted to a glowing screen, and the golden voice of radio now often played in the background, rather than commanding center stage. Despite this cultural shift, radio remained resilient—adapting to cars, clock radios, and eventually digital formats. But for many, the charm of those earlier decades—the weight of a wooden cabinet, the slow sweep of a tuning needle, the faint static that preceded a favorite station—never faded.

Today, vintage radios endure not just as objects of function, but as emblems of a different time. Each one represents a piece of technological progress, a moment of design philosophy, and a unique listening experience. Collectors see more than knobs and tubes—they see the transition from analog curiosity to cultural centerpiece. They hear the echo of Roosevelt's voice, the swing of a Glenn Miller tune, the thrilling urgency of wartime broadcasts. They recognize, within the components, a craftsmanship and intention that's hard to find in the disposable electronics of today.

To understand the value and beauty of a vintage radio, you must first appreciate the journey it's taken—from primitive detectors to glowing tube amplifiers, from hulking wooden consoles to sleek, space-age portables. These devices are not frozen relics. They are milestones in the story of communication, creativity, and connection.

And so, as you begin or continue your journey into the world of vintage radios, know that every dial you turn, every hum you hear, is the product of decades of evolution and ingenuity. The radios we collect today are more than antiques—they are storytellers. They speak not just with sound, but with history. And all you need to do is listen.

Chapter 2: Anatomy of a Vintage Radio

Vintage Radios: A Collector's Guide to Timeless Sound and Style

To truly appreciate a vintage radio is to go beyond its handsome face and listen to the quiet symphony of parts working in perfect harmony beneath the surface. Much like a classic car or a fine mechanical watch, a vintage radio is more than its outer shell—its soul lives inside. That warm hum, the satisfying click of a tuning dial, the amber glow of a vacuum tube—each of these sensory experiences is the result of meticulous engineering. The anatomy of a vintage radio is not just functional, it is a kind of poetry in metal, glass, and wire.

Understanding how these radios work—and what they're made of—opens up a new level of appreciation for collectors. You begin to see not just the style, but the substance. You understand what makes one radio sing and another fall silent. You start to speak the language of coils, tubes, and circuits. Whether your goal is to restore, repair, or simply admire, knowing the anatomy of your vintage radio is the key to unlocking its full charm.

Let's begin with the cabinet—the visible part, the housing that gives each radio its unique personality. Cabinets were once made with the kind of care you'd expect from fine furniture. In the early days, wood was king. Walnut, mahogany, and maple were shaped, carved, and polished into flowing curves and bold silhouettes. Later, during the Art Deco and post-war eras, new materials like Bakelite and early plastics took over, allowing for daring colors and space-age shapes that defined mid-century style. The cabinet isn't just a protective shell—it's the face the radio shows the world, often revealing the era in which it was born.

Inside, the heart of the radio begins with its chassis—the metal frame that holds the entire electronic assembly. Mounted to the chassis are a variety of components that, together, bring sound to life. Chief among them are the tubes—glass cylinders glowing softly when the radio is powered on. These vacuum tubes amplify weak signals into audible sound, functioning much like the muscle in a mechanical system. Each tube is a delicate little factory of electrons, managing the magic of invisible waves and converting them into something human ears can enjoy. Their gentle radiance isn't just nostalgic—it's functional, a sign of life and warmth.

Beside the tubes live the capacitors and resistors, components that regulate electrical flow and help shape the performance of the radio. Coils and transformers manage frequency and voltage, guiding the signal from its raw, invisible state into something ordered and intelligible. These parts, though small, are essential. A failed capacitor or a broken solder joint can silence a radio, reducing it to little more than a decorative relic—until someone with a bit of skill and patience brings it back to life.

Then there's the speaker, where sound finally emerges into the room. Many vintage radios used electromagnetic speakers, which work by moving a paper cone back and forth to produce vibrations in the air. The quality of the speaker, along with the wooden or Bakelite housing around it, deeply affects the warmth and richness of the sound. A well-tuned radio with its original speaker can produce tones that feel remarkably alive, full-bodied in a way that modern speakers rarely replicate.

The tuning mechanism is another marvel. In many radios, a cord-and-pulley system connects the tuning knob to a variable capacitor or inductor. As you turn the dial, you're physically adjusting a component that changes the frequency the radio is tuned to—an elegant, analog act that feels worlds away from digital scanning. The pointer, often lit from behind, glides across the dial scale, bringing you closer to your chosen station with each careful twist.

Now, not all radios are created equal—nor are they powered the same way. One of the key distinctions in vintage radio collecting lies in understanding the difference between tube radios and transistor radios. Tube radios, dominant from the 1920s through the 1950s, are what many collectors think of when imagining a "true" vintage radio. These machines are often larger, heavier, and filled with glowing glass tubes that give them a warm, inviting presence. They require a moment to "warm up" after being turned on—a charming ritual in itself—and they often produce a richer, rounder sound.

Transistor radios, which came into the spotlight in the mid-1950s, revolutionized the industry. Smaller, cooler-running, and more portable, they replaced the bulky vacuum tubes with tiny, solid-state components. A transistor is essentially a miniature amplifier, and radios that used them could fit in a pocket or purse. While many collectors still favor tube radios for their aesthetics and sound, early transistor models are gaining attention for their historical significance and nostalgic appeal. The first generation of transistor radios—especially those made by brands like Regency, Zenith, and Sony—are now highly collectible in their own right.

Knowing what's inside your radio helps you care for it, restore it if needed, and—perhaps most importantly—appreciate it on a deeper level. It changes the way you look at those dials and switches. You begin to understand how the sweep of a needle across a scale is more than just movement—it's an orchestration of parts working together, of sound being drawn from thin air.

To open a vintage radio, whether physically or metaphorically, is to step into a different era of engineering and design. These were devices made to last, built with thoughtfulness, and repaired when broken—not discarded. They came from a time when even the smallest resistor or wire had to be soldered by hand, when design was driven as much by human touch as by electrical necessity.

And so, as you admire your radios—whether they sit quietly on a shelf or sing sweetly from the corner of a room—remember the complexity hidden beneath their elegant shells. Every hum, every whisper, every song they carry is made possible by a symphony of parts working in beautiful harmony. To understand that is to hear them differently. To collect them is not just to preserve objects—but to keep a living art form alive.

Chapter 3: Iconic Styles and Designs

Vintage Radios: A Collector's Guide to Timeless Sound and Style

Before you ever switch on a vintage radio, before the hum of warm tubes or the crackle of distant stations fills the air, there's that moment of admiration—one that starts with the eye. The allure of vintage radios is not limited to the sounds they produce, but to the artistry and design that went into their very shapes, their colors, their presence. These were not just appliances—they were statements. Made to live in the heart of the home, they were meant to be seen, touched, admired. Radios were the centerpieces of mantels, the companions of kitchen counters, the focal points of living rooms, dressed in elegance or adorned with futuristic flair, depending on the decade.

The story of vintage radio design is one of evolving aesthetic tastes, driven by culture, architecture, materials, and the steady march of technology. From the ornate flourishes of the Art Deco era to the sleek, geometric lines of mid-century modernism, each radio is a snapshot of its time. To collect them is not just to collect machines—it's to curate a gallery of visual history.

In the 1930s, as radios began to occupy a more central role in American homes, their designs reflected the grandeur and optimism of the Art Deco movement.

These were radios with presence—bold, symmetrical, and streamlined. You'd find cathedral-style consoles with gothic arches and rounded tops, often made of polished wood that gleamed beneath a living room's lamp light. The dials were often backlit, glowing softly through amber glass or with intricate markings that made tuning feel like navigating a map of sound. These radios weren't shy; they were built to impress. And impress they did, with their rich materials and confident silhouettes standing as symbols of modern luxury.

The 1940s brought a more refined sense of utility. Wartime restrictions on materials meant designers had to get creative, balancing function with form in ways that made radios more compact and accessible. Wood was still common, but so were Bakelite and early plastics—molded into graceful curves or deco-inspired fluting. The emphasis was on reliability, on streamlined shapes that looked clean and modern without veering into extravagance. There's a quiet dignity to 1940s radios—solid, grounded, and subtly elegant.

Then came the 1950s and everything changed. The war was over, optimism was high, and the future was on everyone's mind. This was the era of chrome bumpers, pastel kitchen appliances, and Googie architecture. Radios followed suit. Designers began to break away from the symmetry and restraint of the previous decades, embracing asymmetry, color, and space-age flair. The rise of Bakelite gave way to thermoplastics, allowing radios to be molded in any shape imaginable. You'll see radios in pale pinks and mint greens, others in candy-apple red or bright turquoise, often with metallic accents or sweeping lines that suggest movement even when they're standing still.

By the mid-century mark, the influence of Scandinavian design and modernism was clear. Lines became cleaner, forms more geometric. The 1960s introduced radios that felt more like sculpture than sound machines—boxes with brushed aluminum faces, blocky profiles, or even spherical forms, reflecting the bold experimentation of the Space Age. This was the era when radios looked like something from a science fiction novel. They were not just tools for listening—they were tools for dreaming.

And through it all, certain materials came to define the aesthetics of their time. Bakelite, with its deep swirls and high gloss, became the darling of the 1930s and 40s. Not only was it durable, but it could be molded into smooth, rounded cases that felt satisfying to the touch. Wood, warm and organic, remained a staple—especially in larger console and tabletop models. As plastics improved, they opened up a rainbow of color options, allowing radios to match the era's expanding tastes in interior design.

The dials, too, were a canvas for creativity. Some featured Art Deco numerals, others had luminous hands or radial scales reminiscent of airplane gauges. Logos were often scripted in elegant fonts or stamped in brass, giving each radio a mark of identity and pride. Even the knobs—the simplest of parts—received thoughtful design, with textures and shapes chosen as much for feel as for appearance.

What made these designs iconic wasn't just their beauty—it was their intention. Radio designers were artists and engineers in equal measure. They understood that a radio would become part of a household's landscape, woven into the rhythms of daily life. Its form had to speak to the desires and dreams of the people who owned it. The best of these designs did just that. They weren't merely functional—they were aspirational.

As a collector, one of the great joys lies in recognizing these stylistic shifts and learning to identify the fingerprints of different eras. A smooth Bakelite Emerson in walnut brown tells a different story than a sharp-edged Zenith Trans-Oceanic built like a suitcase for global adventure. A pastel plastic RCA with atomic legs hums a different tune than a towering floor model Philco with a dial the size of a dinner plate.

Some collectors are drawn to the ornate woodwork of cathedral models. Others fall for the candy-colored charm of 1950s tabletops. Some seek minimalism, others opulence. And some, perhaps most delightfully, fall in love with the contrast—displaying a 1930s Deco beauty next to a Sputnik-inspired 1960s oddity, celebrating the breadth of creativity radio design has to offer.

Style matters. Not because it's the only thing—but because it tells us something essential about the people who made and used these radios. It shows us what they valued, how they wanted to live, and what they believed the future could look like. To collect these pieces is to honor that vision, to bring a piece of the past into the present with all its color, warmth, and hope intact.

And so, as you explore vintage radios, don't just look for perfect condition or famous brands. Look for personality. Look for design that speaks to you. Because in this world of dials and knobs, it's not just about what the radio says when it's turned on. It's about what it says before you ever touch it.

Chapter 4: Radio Brands That Made History

Vintage Radios: A Collector's Guide to Timeless Sound and Style

Every collector has their favorites—the brands that call to them, the names that spark nostalgia, admiration, or sheer curiosity. These are the legends, the innovators, the household names that helped shape the radio into what it became: not just a tool for communication, but an icon of technology and design. A nameplate on a radio is more than a label; it's a signature, a story, a stamp of an era. Knowing the makers behind the radios deepens your appreciation and guides your collecting with clarity and purpose.

In America, radio found fertile ground in the early 20th century. Companies sprang up quickly, and by the 1930s, a few had risen to the top—brands like Zenith, RCA, Philco, and Emerson. These names weren't just popular—they were trusted. Families built their daily routines around them. News came through their speakers. Saturday night music programs and wartime broadcasts filled rooms from cabinets bearing these names. And as technology advanced, these companies competed not just to be heard, but to be seen—each striving to produce better performance, more daring design, and stronger emotional connection.

Zenith, for instance, became synonymous with quality and innovation. Their tagline, "The quality goes in before the name goes on," wasn't just a slogan—it was a philosophy. Their radios, especially the famed Trans-Oceanic line, were marvels of engineering and design, capable of pulling in signals from across the globe. Zenith sets often featured bold dials, rich woodwork, and an unmistakable presence. Even today, the name carries weight among collectors.

RCA, the Radio Corporation of America, brought together cutting-edge technology and mass appeal. Their radios were everywhere—from living rooms to schoolrooms to military installations. RCA helped define the golden age of radio, blending technical innovation with a keen sense for market trends. Their designs were often forward-thinking, stylish without being showy, and their build quality was consistently strong.

Philco, short for Philadelphia Storage Battery Company, carved its own niche with sleek, elegant models that balanced affordability with style. Their "cathedral" and "bullet" models are highly sought after today, their shapes and finishes capturing the spirit of the 1930s and 40s perfectly. Philco was known not just for aesthetics, but also for pioneering advancements in radio circuitry and engineering.

Then there was Emerson, a brand that embraced change and chased innovation with enthusiasm. Emerson was one of the first companies to fully embrace the shift from tube to transistor, and they weren't afraid to explore bold new forms and materials. Their radios were often smaller, more affordable, and stylishly modern—perfect for a postwar generation hungry for sleek design and portable convenience.

Crossing the Atlantic, Europe had its own giants—brands that brought an entirely different sensibility to radio design. In Germany, Grundig and Telefunken were powerhouses. Their radios, particularly from the 1950s and 60s, are revered for their refined tone, incredible craftsmanship, and restrained elegance. Many featured warm wooden cabinets with delicate veneers, gold accents, and multi-band capabilities that allowed users to listen to stations from across the world. These were radios for serious listeners—technically sophisticated, acoustically rich, and beautifully made.

Telefunken, with its roots deep in the early days of wireless communication, became a benchmark for high-fidelity sound. Their radios often featured multiple speakers, intricate tuning dials, and push-button band selectors—creating an experience that felt both modern and luxurious. Collectors value Telefunken radios not only for their performance but for the sheer quality of their construction.

Grundig followed a similar path, with a flair for both form and function. Their radios from the 1950s are particularly beloved, combining rounded lines, subtle details, and excellent engineering. Listening to a well-preserved Grundig today feels like stepping into a gentler, more refined world—a quiet evening, a jazz station faintly tuned in from another country, and the warm resonance of expertly crafted speakers.

Across the channel, British brands like Bush and Roberts brought their own sensibilities to the scene. Bush radios are prized for their quirky charm and colorful styling, particularly the iconic DAC90A model—a curvy, cheerful set that's become a symbol of post-war British design. Roberts, on the other hand, leaned toward portability and refinement. Their small, leather-clad radios from the 1950s and 60s were both fashionable and functional, combining high-quality sound with the sort of charm that made them feel like accessories as much as electronics.

And then there was Japan. In the 1950s and 60s, Japanese manufacturers burst onto the scene with revolutionary transistor technology and bold new approaches to portability. Sony, in particular, became a global powerhouse with the introduction of the TR-63—the world's first truly pocket-sized transistor radio. Suddenly, radios weren't just for the home. They were for your coat pocket, your beach bag, your dashboard. The design was compact, futuristic, and fun.

Panasonic, too, played a major role in reshaping radio design. Their transistor sets often combined stylish lines with clever features and excellent reliability. While these Japanese models may not carry the old-world romance of wood and tubes, they represent a turning point in radio history—one that embraced youth culture, mobility, and mass appeal.

What makes a brand collectible? It's not just the age or the rarity. It's the legacy. It's the way a radio from a certain maker reflects the spirit of its time. It's the consistency of quality, the inventiveness of design, the way it makes you feel when you turn the knob and hear a station fade into focus. Some brands built reputations on power and range. Others leaned into elegance or affordability. And some—like Sony and Zenith—reshaped the entire idea of what a radio could be.

For collectors, brand awareness adds a new layer to the hobby. You begin to spot patterns: the symmetrical dials of Philcos, the gold-trimmed faces of Grundigs, the playful colors of mid-century RCAs. You learn to trust certain names, to recognize quality at a glance. You also develop favorites—not necessarily based on value, but on connection. Maybe it's the radio that sat on your grandparents' kitchen counter. Maybe it's a design you've only seen in pictures, but can't stop thinking about.

That's the magic of these brands. They aren't just manufacturers. They're storytellers. They built more than machines—they built icons, moments, and memories. When you collect vintage radios, you're not just gathering objects. You're curating voices from the past, each one marked with a name that once meant reliability, beauty, innovation, or maybe just a few quiet moments by the glow of a tuning dial. And those names, still etched onto metal plates and plastic faceplates decades later, continue to speak.

Chapter 5: Collecting with Confidence

Vintage Radios: A Collector's Guide to Timeless Sound and Style

Starting a collection of vintage radios can feel like stepping into a beautifully lit antique shop where every object whispers a story, each dial seems to wink with secrets, and each cabinet hums with history. There's a magic to the hunt, a thrill in the discovery, and a quiet satisfaction in bringing home a new piece to add to your growing chorus of timeworn voices. But beyond the charm and nostalgia, collecting wisely—and with confidence—requires a bit of know-how, a trained eye, and, perhaps most importantly, a sense of purpose.

Many collectors begin their journey with a spark: a radio found in a dusty corner of a thrift store, a piece inherited from a grandparent's attic, or a sudden admiration sparked by the graceful curve of a Bakelite case in a vintage photograph. Whatever the starting point, the path forward quickly branches into exciting, sometimes overwhelming terrain. There are hundreds of models, countless manufacturers, subtle variations in dials and trim, and a wide range of conditions and values. The question is no longer just *"Do I love this?"*—but also *"Is it authentic?"*, *"Is it original?"*, and *"Is it worth it?"*

To collect with confidence means to develop your ability to discern. It means learning to see beyond surface charm and understanding what gives a radio its historical, aesthetic, and mechanical value. A genuine vintage radio—especially one that is original and well-preserved—holds a kind of integrity that's instantly recognizable once you've seen enough of them. The materials will feel honest. The wear will tell a believable story. The screws and knobs and labels will feel right, not out of place or artificially aged.

Start by examining details. The dial face, for instance, often reveals more than you'd expect. Is the lettering sharp and era-appropriate? Are the markings consistent with the brand and model year? Does the tuning pointer appear original, or does it seem like a modern replacement? Flip the radio around and check the back. Many vintage models still carry their original paper labels, model numbers, or patent information. These little clues are invaluable—reference points that can help you verify authenticity, date of manufacture, and even the radio's place in the brand's lineup.

Then there's the matter of Franken-radios. These are radios that have been cobbled together from different parts—perhaps with a cabinet from one model, a dial from another, and internals from yet another. While some Franken-radios are charming curiosities, others can be misleading or misrepresented. Sometimes it's an honest attempt at restoration. Other times it's an effort to pass off something more valuable than it really is. Either way, it pays to do your homework. Compare your finds to catalogs, collector guides, and trusted online resources. When in doubt, ask other collectors. Most are more than happy to share their knowledge and help you avoid a costly mistake.

Equally important to authenticity is originality. A radio may be genuine, but has it been altered? Has the cabinet been refinished, the dial replaced, or the electronics modernized? While there's nothing inherently wrong with tasteful restoration, a radio in untouched, all-original condition will generally be more desirable to collectors. Patina, when it's natural and well-earned, is a badge of honor. A few scuffs on the Bakelite, a slight yellowing of the dial glass—these are the fingerprints of time, and they often add to a piece's story and charm.

Of course, part of collecting with confidence is knowing yourself—understanding what you want your collection to be. Some collectors chase rarity, assembling a catalog of scarce or high-value pieces. Others are driven by design, curating a visual timeline of styles and materials. And still others follow sentiment, collecting models from specific years or brands that hold personal meaning. There's no right or wrong approach. But having a guiding philosophy helps you collect with intention rather than impulse. It helps you say "yes" or "no" with clarity and excitement, rather than hesitation or regret.

The process of growing a collection also sharpens your instincts. The more radios you see—whether in person, in catalogs, or online—the more fluent you become in their language. You'll start recognizing model lines, spotting uncommon variants, and identifying subtle cues that differentiate early and late production runs. Your hands will learn the feel of original knobs, your eyes will catch details others might miss, and your gut will guide you toward the radios that matter most to you.

And yet, even seasoned collectors make mistakes. A radio that looks stunning in a photo may arrive with hairline cracks or hidden damage. An eBay deal that seemed too good to be true might, in fact, be just that. But these bumps are part of the journey. They teach you resilience, deepen your appreciation, and often lead you to better discoveries down the line. Each misstep sharpens your future decisions and gives your collection a sense of hard-earned wisdom.

Collecting vintage radios is not about perfection—it's about connection. It's about finding pieces that speak to you, pieces that carry echoes of voices and music once transmitted through thin air into living rooms, kitchens, and bedrooms. It's about honoring the past by preserving it, celebrating the beauty of analog design, and participating in a tradition of appreciation that spans generations.

So trust your eye. Train your hand. Follow your curiosity. And collect with confidence—not because you know everything, but because you're willing to learn, to listen, and to love the stories these radios carry. Over time, your collection won't just grow in size—it will grow in meaning, becoming a reflection of your taste, your values, and your journey through the beautiful, humming world of vintage sound.

Chapter 6: Valuation and Rarity

Vintage Radios: A Collector's Guide to Timeless Sound and Style

There comes a moment in every collector's journey when sentiment meets curiosity, and curiosity gives way to a question that feels both exciting and a little daunting: *What is it worth?* That moment can arise when you stumble upon a dusty tabletop model at a flea market, when a friend hands you a hand-me-down Philco, or when your growing collection starts to demand its own display cabinet. Whatever the spark, the question of value eventually finds its way into the conversation. And rightly so—because vintage radios, for all their nostalgia and beauty, are also collectible artifacts, each with a market value shaped by a delicate mix of condition, rarity, provenance, and desirability.

But valuation isn't a formula. It's not a matter of plugging numbers into an equation and getting a hard answer. Rather, it's a nuanced practice that blends history with instinct, research with observation. To understand what a vintage radio is worth, you first have to understand what makes it rare, what makes it special, and—perhaps most importantly—what makes it desirable to others. Because in the end, value is not just about what something cost when it was new. It's about what someone is willing to pay for it now, in its current condition, in the context of a changing collector's market.

Rarity is often the first quality people associate with value, and it certainly plays a role. A radio that was produced in small quantities or was only sold in a specific region may be harder to find today, and therefore more sought after. But rarity alone doesn't guarantee high value. Some rare radios may have limited appeal due to their design, technical limitations, or brand recognition. Others may be rare simply because they were unsuccessful when new—and remain underappreciated now.

Condition, on the other hand, is a far more reliable indicator of value. Originality matters. A radio that has all its original components, from the knobs and dial face to the back panel and internal circuitry, will always hold more value than one that has been heavily modified or poorly restored. Collectors prize authenticity. Chips, cracks, missing parts, or amateur repairs can significantly lower a radio's worth. Conversely, a well-preserved example, even if not especially rare, can command a surprising price simply because of its pristine condition.

Then there's the matter of brand and model. Certain names—Zenith, Philco, RCA, Grundig, Telefunken—carry a prestige that often translates into higher value. Within each brand, specific models have emerged as icons, cherished for their design, performance, or historical relevance. The Zenith Trans-Oceanic series, for instance, remains consistently desirable among collectors due to its international reception capability and rugged elegance. Philco's "cathedral" radios of the 1930s are similarly prized, both for their distinctive style and their role in American radio history.

A radio's design can also be a major factor in valuation. Collectors and decorators alike gravitate toward Art Deco and mid-century modern styles. A radio that features striking materials—deeply swirled Bakelite, bright plastic in bold colors, or intricate wooden inlays—can often fetch more simply for its aesthetic appeal. Some radios straddle both worlds, offering both beautiful design and technical innovation, which makes them especially desirable. These are the models that tend to appreciate steadily over time, admired both by audiophiles and those with an eye for vintage decor.

Provenance, while more difficult to verify, adds a rich layer of interest—and sometimes value. A radio with a documented history, perhaps one used by a well-known individual or kept in a specific public space, can become a collector's prize. Even a handwritten note inside the cabinet, an old service sticker, or a receipt tucked in the back panel can add to the story and charm of the piece, increasing its sentimental and collectible value.

So how does one go about determining what a specific radio is worth? The first step is research. Auction archives, collector forums, vintage electronics websites, and price guides offer a helpful starting point. Comparing recent sales of the same model in similar condition can give you a sense of the going rate. But remember that markets shift. What was valuable ten years ago may be less so today, and what's obscure now may catch fire next year thanks to a viral video or design trend.

Photography and presentation also matter. If you're looking to appraise or sell a radio, how you present it can affect perception—and therefore value. Clean it gently. Photograph it well, with good lighting and from multiple angles. Show the details that matter: the dial, the brand logo, the tubes (if visible), and any markings or labels. Be honest about its condition, but also highlight its strengths. A radio that tells a clear story—through both images and words—tends to draw more interest and command a higher price.

For formal appraisals, you might consider consulting a professional. Antique dealers, auction houses, or appraisers who specialize in vintage electronics can provide expert opinions, often backed by market data and experience. This is especially useful if you're looking to insure a high-value piece or plan to sell at auction. A professional appraisal adds credibility and reassurance for both buyer and seller.

It's also worth noting that the value of a radio is not always monetary. For many collectors, the real worth lies in the connection—a childhood memory, a link to a specific era, or simply the joy of reviving a forgotten voice from the past. Some radios may never sell for much, but they earn a treasured place on the shelf all the same. And that's a kind of value that no price tag can capture.

Still, understanding the financial landscape of vintage radio collecting helps you become a more informed, more confident collector. It allows you to make wise purchases, to spot a true bargain or walk away from an overpriced find. It empowers you to grow your collection with care and clarity, balancing passion with prudence.

As you continue your journey, keep your eyes open not just for what's rare or expensive, but for what's special—what resonates with you, what adds depth to your collection, what brings history alive in your hands. Because in the world of vintage radios, value isn't found in the dollars alone. It's found in the stories we preserve, the beauty we admire, and the voices we bring back to life, one radio at a time.

Chapter 7: Restoration and Repair

Vintage Radios: A Collector's Guide to Timeless Sound and Style

There's something profoundly satisfying about turning the dial on a vintage radio and hearing the warm crackle of sound fade into clarity. When a radio that hasn't spoken in decades finally comes to life again—when the tubes glow, the speaker hums, and distant music trickles through—it feels like magic. But the truth is, that magic often requires a little help. Restoration and repair are essential parts of collecting vintage radios, not only for keeping these beautiful objects functional, but for honoring their history and craftsmanship in the process.

To restore a vintage radio is to step into the role of caretaker. You're not just polishing a case or replacing a tube—you're reviving a story. Whether your goal is a full restoration or gentle preservation, the choices you make during this process matter. They shape how the radio will look, sound, and endure for years to come. The key is to approach the task with reverence, curiosity, and a commitment to doing no harm.

The first step is understanding what you have. Before reaching for a screwdriver, take time to research your radio's make, model, and history. Examine the cabinet, the dial, the back panel, and especially the chassis inside. Look for original labels, serial numbers, or manufacturing stamps. These clues help you date the radio, identify its components, and make informed decisions about what should be restored—and what should be left as-is.

It's tempting, especially for newcomers, to want everything to look "like new." But part of a vintage radio's charm is the passage of time. That worn volume knob, the gentle discoloration around the dial, the patina on the speaker grill—these are not flaws. They're signatures. They tell the story of a radio that's lived, one that's sat on mantels, filled rooms with music, and maybe even delivered wartime broadcasts or Sunday jazz. When considering restoration, always ask: Am I preserving history, or erasing it?

Cleaning is usually the safest and most rewarding place to begin. A gentle dusting, a careful wipe with a damp cloth, perhaps a polish of the Bakelite or wood—these small acts can transform a neglected radio into a display-worthy piece without disturbing its originality. Avoid harsh chemicals and abrasive materials. Use soft brushes, microfiber cloths, and mild soap if needed. When dealing with wood cabinets, a quality wood polish or conditioner can bring back the richness of grain without altering the finish.

Inside the radio, things become more delicate. If you're new to electronics, resist the urge to tinker beyond what you understand. The electrical components inside vintage tube radios—capacitors, resistors, transformers—can degrade over time, and some may even pose safety hazards. Replacing old paper capacitors or failed electrolytics is often necessary for proper function, but should be done carefully and with respect for the original layout. When possible, source period-correct components, or hide modern replacements in vintage-style shells to preserve the look of the chassis.

If you do venture into electronic repair, take your time. Use a variac (variable AC power supply) to power up the radio slowly, watching for signs of trouble. If the tubes light up and the radio hums but doesn't receive stations, it could be a simple alignment issue or a weak tube. But always remember: high voltages can linger inside even an unplugged radio. If you're unsure, consult a professional.

Professional restorers, especially those who specialize in antique electronics, are invaluable partners in this journey. They can diagnose subtle issues, replace hard-to-find components, and restore performance without compromising authenticity. A good restorer respects both the technical and aesthetic aspects of vintage radios. They'll work with you to decide what should be repaired, what can be preserved, and how to balance originality with usability.

And then there's the dial—arguably the soul of the radio. Faded, cracked, or damaged dial glass can sometimes be replaced, but many collectors prefer to keep the original even if imperfect. Reproductions are available for some popular models, but nothing quite matches the charm of aged paint and softly glowing numerals that have guided countless fingers to music and news over the years.

Knobs, grills, and back panels are also frequent casualties of time. Luckily, the vintage radio community is generous and resourceful. Online forums, collector groups, and specialized suppliers often carry reproduction parts, or even original spares sourced from "parts sets" beyond repair. Swapping in missing or damaged pieces from the same model is generally accepted in the hobby, especially when it helps restore a radio to its former glory.

That said, be cautious with over-restoration. Too much polish, too many modern modifications, or aggressive refinishing can strip away the soul of a vintage piece. A 1940s radio that looks like it just rolled off the assembly line might catch the eye, but to seasoned collectors, it can feel hollow—like a painting that's been repainted too many times. The goal is to preserve the spirit of the original, not to disguise its age.

One of the most beautiful things about restoring vintage radios is how it connects you to the hands that built them, the ears that listened to them, and the moments they carried. You'll find yourself appreciating the tiny details—a perfectly balanced tuning dial, the glow of a tube on a quiet evening, the surprising richness of sound from a speaker that predates color television. These experiences are the reward for your care, your patience, and your attention.

Whether you're meticulously restoring a high-end Zenith console or gently coaxing life back into a humble plastic transistor set, the process is deeply personal. It's a conversation between you and the past, one in which your hands bring something old back into the present, ready to sing again. And when it does—when that first station fades in, or the dial lights up for the first time in years—you'll know that your work wasn't just about repair. It was about revival.

So take your time. Learn the craft. Ask for help. And enjoy the process. Because in the world of vintage radios, every scratch has a story, every hum a heartbeat, and every restoration a small but meaningful act of preservation.

Chapter 8: Displaying and Preserving Your Collection

Vintage Radios: A Collector's Guide to Timeless Sound and Style

There comes a moment in every collector's journey when the radios start to speak even when they're not playing. Arranged thoughtfully on shelves or sitting proudly on tables, their silent presence tells stories of design, history, and craftsmanship. A well-displayed vintage radio doesn't just look beautiful—it resonates with meaning. It becomes a sculptural object, a talking piece, a subtle pulse of the past woven into the fabric of a room.

The way we display our radios reflects not only our personal style but also how much we respect and cherish the objects themselves. Some collectors prefer minimalist arrangements—one radio, perfectly spotlighted, occupying a place of honor. Others lean into abundance, curating entire walls of colorful Bakelite sets, or crafting mid-century vignettes complete with vintage furniture and accessories to set the scene. There is no right or wrong approach. The key is intentionality—placing each piece in a way that allows it to be seen, appreciated, and protected.

Start by considering your environment. Radios are surprisingly sensitive to their surroundings, especially those with wood cabinets or delicate electronics. Direct sunlight, high humidity, and temperature fluctuations can quietly wreak havoc on even the sturdiest of sets. Over time, ultraviolet rays can fade dial markings and discolor plastics. Humidity can cause wood to warp or veneers to lift. Dust, when allowed to settle into speaker grilles or control knobs, can become a grimy layer that dulls both appearance and performance.

The best displays combine aesthetics with protection. Choose a location that avoids harsh direct sunlight and is well-ventilated but not overly drafty. If you're using shelves, make sure they're sturdy and level—some of these radios, especially console or cathedral models, can be surprisingly heavy and require solid support. Consider using felt or soft pads under the radios to prevent scuffing and to allow airflow underneath.

Grouping radios by style, era, or color can create a beautiful visual rhythm. A row of 1950s pastel plastics lined along a narrow shelf can feel whimsical and bright. A cluster of wooden 1930s cathedral models on a credenza might feel warm and reverent. Mixing styles and decades works, too, if done thoughtfully—contrast creates conversation. A shiny red transistor beside a walnut tube set tells a story of evolution. The key is balance, space, and a willingness to let each radio speak its piece.

Lighting plays a powerful role in display. A small spotlight or warm-toned lamp aimed just right can enhance the curves of a cabinet, the glow of a dial, or the texture of old lacquer. Avoid harsh, cool lighting that can flatten a radio's features. The goal is ambiance—light that flatters, not overwhelms. If you're displaying a working radio, let it glow now and then. A warm backlit dial in the evening creates a nostalgic atmosphere that no modern smart speaker can replicate.

For larger collections, glass-front display cabinets offer both beauty and protection. They keep dust at bay, allow for tiered arrangements, and lend a museum-like quality that suits particularly rare or fragile pieces. Inside a cabinet, risers and stands can help elevate smaller sets, allowing every piece its moment in the spotlight. Labeling, while not necessary, can also add an informative touch, especially if you're sharing your collection with others or simply enjoy noting the year, brand, or model of each piece.

Preservation, though, goes beyond display. It's about caring for your collection with long-term stewardship in mind. Even radios that aren't in working condition deserve thoughtful handling. Avoid stacking them unless they're built for it, and be cautious when moving them—some older Bakelite cases can crack under pressure or stress, and wood joints may be more fragile than they appear.

Routine maintenance is an important part of preservation. Dust your radios gently and regularly with a soft cloth or brush. For hard-to-reach places—between grill slats or around knobs—a small, clean makeup brush or camera lens brush can work wonders. Avoid household cleaners, which may damage finishes or lettering. For radios with glass dials or windows, a lightly dampened microfiber cloth is usually enough. If you ever need to clean inside the chassis or speaker area, be extremely cautious—or leave it to a professional.

If your radios are functional, consider running them occasionally. Letting a tube radio sit unused for years can actually hasten its decline. Like old cars, they often do best when exercised gently from time to time. Just be sure you're doing so safely, especially with radios that haven't been electrically restored. Using a variac to slowly power up an older set, or at least plugging it into a surge protector, can help reduce the risk of damage.

Cataloging your collection may seem like a task for the deeply committed, but it's a rewarding practice for any collector. Keeping a simple inventory—notes on model numbers, condition, date of acquisition, or even where the radio was found—adds a layer of meaning and continuity to your collection. It also becomes invaluable if you ever choose to downsize, donate, or pass your collection along. Some collectors go further, photographing each radio, writing short histories, or even creating custom display tags. These little acts elevate your collection from a private passion to a curated archive of radio history.

Ultimately, how you display and preserve your vintage radios is an extension of your relationship with them. It's a form of storytelling. These radios, after all, once belonged to someone else. They lived in other homes, played songs you've never heard, delivered news that changed the world. By caring for them now—by giving them a home, a space, a spotlight—you're keeping those voices alive.

In your display, there's room for reverence and playfulness, for design and function, for silence and sound. A vintage radio, placed thoughtfully, becomes more than décor. It becomes a window into another time, a symbol of endurance, and a tribute to the enduring beauty of analog sound. Whether you have two radios or twenty, whether they work or simply watch over your living room like graceful sentinels, display them proudly. Care for them gently. Let them be what they are: stories you can touch, music you can see, and timeless reminders that even in a digital world, the old ways still have something beautiful to say.

Chapter 9: Buying and Selling Vintage Radios

Vintage Radios: A Collector's Guide to Timeless Sound and Style

There's a certain thrill in the hunt—whether it's spotting a dusty gem tucked behind a stack of magazines at a flea market or watching the final seconds tick down on an online auction for a model you've been chasing for years. Buying vintage radios is as much about the story of the find as it is about the radio itself. Likewise, selling a vintage piece can be an act of passing on history, of letting go with purpose, of knowing that something meaningful will find a new life in someone else's collection.

The world of buying and selling vintage radios is both exhilarating and unpredictable. One moment you're negotiating over a tabletop RCA in someone's garage; the next, you're clicking through meticulously curated listings on a collector's website. There's no single best place to buy or sell—only a variety of doors into this shared love of sound and design. Each has its own rhythm, its own rules, and its own unique sense of possibility.

Estate sales and garage sales are often the most romanticized—and for good reason. There's something deeply personal about finding a radio in someone's home, surrounded by the echoes of its original life. Often these radios haven't been moved in decades. The dial may still be set to a long-forgotten station. The cabinet may still hold the warmth of the room it once called home. Prices here can be unpredictable. Some sellers see an old radio and slap on a bargain-bin price tag, unaware of what they're letting go. Others Google a few keywords and price their dusty Crosley as if it belonged in a museum. Politeness, patience, and a friendly conversation can go a long way toward bridging that gap.

Flea markets and antique malls offer their own kind of magic. The volume of items and sellers means more chances to stumble upon a treasure—and more opportunities to haggle. Here, cash is still king, and deals are often made on instinct. A collector with a sharp eye and a well-trained sense of authenticity can walk away with incredible finds. Still, it's easy to be caught up in the moment. A radio that seems charming on a shelf under the glare of overhead lights might not look quite as appealing once you get it home and notice the missing knobs or a hairline crack in the case. Always take your time. Inspect. Ask questions. Trust your gut.

Auctions—whether live or online—are where passion meets adrenaline. Bidding on a rare Zenith or a mint condition Telefunken can feel like stepping into an arena. Emotions run high, competition can be fierce, and it's easy to get swept up in the thrill. But auctions also offer access to radios that rarely surface elsewhere, and the opportunity to see what other collectors are willing to pay can be incredibly educational. Sites like eBay still serve as a global marketplace for vintage radios, offering variety and reach, though they require a careful eye. Photographs can be misleading. Descriptions can be vague. Look for sellers with strong reputations, clear communication, and a track record of honest transactions.

Then there are the hidden corners of the internet—the forums, niche collector sites, social media groups—where the vintage radio community thrives in conversation, trade, and camaraderie. These places aren't just marketplaces; they're ecosystems. Buying here often feels more like a shared celebration than a transaction. People post radios not just to sell them, but to find them good homes. Stories are shared, advice is exchanged, and sometimes, trades are made without a dollar ever changing hands. If you're looking for a deeper connection to the hobby and its people, this is where you'll find it.

When it comes to selling, presentation is everything. A radio you've cared for deserves to be shown in its best light. Clean it gently. Photograph it from every angle. Show the details: the dial, the brand, the knobs, the back panel, even the internals if safely accessible. A well-lit, clutter-free backdrop elevates your listing instantly. Include as much information as you can: make, model, year (if known), condition, any restorations done, and whether it's in working order. Transparency builds trust—and trust moves radios from one collector to another with respect and joy.

Pricing can be tricky. The temptation to aim high is natural, especially if you've poured time and effort into restoration or if the radio carries sentimental weight. But remember, value in the marketplace is shaped by demand, not just desire. Research similar sales. Consider the rarity, condition, and functionality of your piece. If you're unsure, start with a fair asking price and be open to negotiation. Many sellers find that their best results come not from pricing for maximum profit, but from pricing for connection—the joy of knowing their piece will be truly appreciated.

Packing and shipping, while less glamorous, is a crucial part of selling. Radios are fragile, and nothing ruins a sale faster than a beautiful Bakelite set arriving in pieces. Use generous padding—bubble wrap, foam, and double boxing if necessary. Remove any loose parts or tubes before shipping and wrap them separately. Label the box as fragile and consider insuring high-value shipments. Selling is more than just moving an item—it's sending a piece of history across space to continue its journey.

Perhaps the most beautiful aspect of buying and selling vintage radios is how cyclical it is. One person's find becomes another's treasure. A forgotten console is rediscovered, restored, and displayed once again. Radios move from collector to collector, passing through homes and hands, each time adding another layer to their story. They're not static artifacts—they're living history, reawakened with every new owner, every careful tune of the dial.

So whether you're buying your very first radio or selling one you've lovingly restored, do it with intention. Let the process be guided not just by profit or acquisition, but by passion. Be the kind of buyer who asks questions, who honors the object. Be the kind of seller who shares stories, who passes along a piece of the past with care. In doing so, you'll discover that buying and selling vintage radios is more than a transaction—it's a tradition, a conversation, and a way of keeping timeless sound and style alive for generations to come.

Chapter 10: The Vintage Radio Community and Resources

Vintage Radios: A Collector's Guide to Timeless Sound and Style

Collecting vintage radios may begin as a solitary pursuit—a quiet fascination with wood grain, a fondness for the soft glow of a dial, or a curiosity sparked by an old box discovered in an attic—but it rarely stays that way. The deeper you go, the more you realize you're not alone. All across the world, there are people just like you: listeners, restorers, admirers, storytellers—each of them drawn to the hum and heartbeat of the past. And together, they've built something wonderful: a vibrant, generous, and ever-growing community where knowledge is shared, passions are kindled, and radios continue to speak, even in silence.

The vintage radio community is not confined to one place or one platform. It lives in real-life clubs and digital forums, in museum archives and hobbyist blogs, in YouTube repair tutorials and weekend swap meets. It thrives wherever someone cares enough to ask, "Does anyone recognize this model?" or "How do I fix this tuning dial?" or simply, "Isn't this beautiful?" That shared appreciation forms the heart of the community. And whether you're a beginner seeking advice or a seasoned collector eager to mentor, there's a seat at the table for you.

One of the most enduring aspects of this world is the presence of collector clubs. Many of these groups have been around for decades, formed by enthusiasts long before social media gave hobbyists a global platform. Organizations like the Antique Wireless Association, the Vintage Radio and Phonograph Society, and the California Historical Radio Society offer everything from educational resources to newsletters, swap meets, and annual conventions. Joining one of these clubs opens the door to a wealth of knowledge, hands-on events, and a sense of belonging that transcends geography and experience level.

Within these clubs, members exchange not only radios and parts but wisdom and stories. There's something special about talking to someone who's been restoring old sets since the 1970s, someone who remembers using a Zenith Trans-Oceanic during their Navy service, or someone who can identify a rare model just by the shape of its knobs. These are the keepers of oral history, the living encyclopedias who help make vintage radio collecting not just a hobby, but a tradition.

Online forums are equally invaluable. Sites like the Antique Radio Forums (antiqueradios.com) offer active communities where questions are asked, advice is given freely, and discoveries are celebrated. Whether you're trying to date a European table radio, troubleshoot a weak speaker, or figure out how to re-string a tuning dial, chances are someone has done it—and is happy to walk you through it. The tone of these spaces is often warm and welcoming, with a shared understanding that everyone started somewhere, and that learning is part of the joy.

Social media, too, has become a powerful tool for connection. Facebook groups, Instagram accounts, and YouTube channels have brought collectors together in real time. A post about a new find can spark a flood of comments, insights, or even new friendships. Watching someone breathe life into a long-silent radio through a restoration video or seeing a perfectly curated display of colorful 1950s sets in someone's home halfway across the world is both inspiring and unifying. The vintage radio world is no longer limited by distance or time zones—it lives in your pocket, ready to welcome you in.

For those eager to dive deeper into the history and mechanics of radios, museums and historical archives provide a rich and immersive experience. Institutions like the AWA Museum in Bloomfield, New York, or the Radio Museum in Fürth, Germany, preserve and display some of the finest and rarest examples of radio technology from around the world. These places aren't just for looking—they're for learning. Exhibits often include background on inventors, broadcasting history, and the societal impact of radio. For collectors, they offer inspiration, perspective, and context—reminders that these objects we collect were once part of something much larger.

Books, too, remain a timeless and tactile resource. While the internet is fast and expansive, there's something grounding about flipping through a printed volume filled with diagrams, advertisements, and essays from radio's golden age. Titles like *The Zenith Trans-Oceanic: The Royalty of Radios* or *Classic Radio: Big Band Years* give collectors historical depth, technical guidance, and a sense of continuity with earlier generations of radio lovers. Even out-of-print guides, found at library sales or online marketplaces, can hold treasures of knowledge you won't find anywhere else.

And let's not forget podcasts and online interviews, which bring voices—both literal and metaphorical—back into the world of radio. Listening to a conversation between two collectors, or hearing a retired engineer talk about the sets they built decades ago, feels like sitting around a campfire where stories are passed down, one signal at a time. These resources make radio collecting feel alive and evolving, rather than frozen in time.

Perhaps the greatest resource of all, though, is conversation. Ask questions. Share your passion. Talk to the person behind the antique shop counter, the older gentleman at the swap meet, the Instagram collector who shares daily photos. The vintage radio community, for all its reverence of the past, is built on connection in the present. The more you engage, the more you'll find that your appreciation deepens—not just for the radios themselves, but for the people who keep them alive.

In this age of instant everything, the world of vintage radios invites us to slow down, to listen closely, and to be part of a story still being written. It's a world full of gentle clicks and glowing dials, of laughter over long-distance trades and advice typed out in the early hours of the morning. It's a world where the sound of an old speaker coming to life brings a smile not just to your face, but to others across towns, countries, and continents.

So as you continue your journey, know that you're not doing it alone. You're walking among thousands of others who find joy in the same hums, the same static, the same soft glow of vacuum tubes. And every time you share a photo, ask a question, or tell someone about the first time you heard a vintage radio come alive, you help that world grow a little larger—and a little louder.

Collecting vintage radios is about more than things. It's about people. It's about community. And that, perhaps, is the clearest signal of all.

Conclusion

Vintage Radios: A Collector's Guide to Timeless Sound and Style

As you reach the end of this guide, you've traveled through more than a century of innovation, design, and sound. You've stepped into the wood-paneled living rooms of the 1930s, felt the pulse of mid-century modern style, and followed the hum of tubes and transistors through the decades. But beyond the facts, the models, and the restoration tips, what you've really explored is a world of stories—one where voices and melodies once drifted through rooms and across continents, carried on waves invisible but unforgettable.

To collect vintage radios is to become part of those stories. You are not merely gathering objects—you are preserving the echoes of generations. You are holding in your hands the very machines that once brought wartime broadcasts to anxious families, that played swing music through summer evenings, that delivered breaking news and bedtime tales and the soundtrack of ordinary life. These radios are more than relics. They are vessels of human experience, frozen in Bakelite, wood, and brass, and brought back to life each time you turn the dial.

There's a quiet kind of joy in this pursuit. The joy of discovery, when a forgotten set reveals itself behind a row of dusty books. The joy of revival, when a silent cabinet once again crackles to life. And the joy of connection—when your collection sparks a conversation, a memory, a sense of shared appreciation with someone who remembers when these machines were not antiques, but companions.

And yet, collecting vintage radios isn't about quantity. It's about intention. It's about finding what speaks to you—whether it's a sleek transistor from the Space Age or a grand cathedral console from the Great Depression. It's about curating a collection that reflects your tastes, your values, your curiosity. And it's about sharing that passion with others, whether through stories, restoration, or simply by letting someone hear the warm tone of a tube radio for the first time.

As you continue on this journey—whether you're just starting your first collection or expanding a long-standing one—let your love for these timeless machines guide you. Stay curious. Stay respectful of the history in your hands. And never underestimate the power of listening—not just to the radios themselves, but to the people and memories they still connect us to.

In a world increasingly driven by fleeting digital noise, vintage radios offer something rare: permanence, presence, and a chance to pause. They remind us that sound once mattered differently, that craftsmanship had soul, and that even silence, framed by a glowing dial, can be profound.

So tune in. Listen closely. The past still has something beautiful to say—and you are now one of the lucky few who knows how to hear it.

Printed in Dunstable, United Kingdom

70720819R10037